The PeaceFinder

Riley McFee's Quest
for World Peace

Including a Special Section on
The Eight Steps to World Peace:
A Handbook for PeaceFinders (That's You!)

Joan McWilliams

Illustrated by
Shannon Parish

The PeaceFinder: Riley McFee's Quest for World Peace

Text and Illustration Copyright © 2006 Joan McWilliams

All rights reserved.

PUBLISHED BY

Balue Fox Publishing Company
P.O. Box 61097
Denver, CO 80206

First Edition.

ISBN-10: 0-9768663-1-5
ISBN-13: 978-0-9768663-1-2

Library of Congress Control Number: 2005904326

The author is grateful for the permission to use the quote from Margaret Mead, courtesy of the Institute of International Studies, Inc., New York.

Printed and bound in Canada
10   9   8   7   6   5   4   3   2   1   0

The origami crane is a symbol of
international peace. According to an ancient
Japanese legend, if you make 1,000 cranes,
your wish for peace will come true.
If you want to make your own peace cranes,
you will find instructions in
Step Eight of the Handbook on page 98.

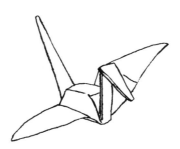

*This book is dedicated
with unqualified love to
Riley and Cory,
Jacques and Balue,
and my wonderful husband, Bob.*

Contents

From the Author

*I*n the summer of 2002, I realized that, regardless of any arguments to the contrary, the United States would invade Iraq. I could hardly believe that, after all the brutality the world has suffered, we had not learned how to resolve problems without bloodshed.

My sheer and utter frustration led me to question my role in this morass. Feeling totally inadequate, I asked, "What could I do to stop violence? What could I do to contribute to world peace?" My answer came the next morning. The clear and unequivocal message was, "Write a book!"

I took that message to heart and, true to my legal training, began to research the subject. I read everything I could—from global consciousness to quantum theory. My goal was to find a way for people to join their thoughts and create world peace. I anticipated that, if I *could* find an answer, it would be very complicated and difficult to understand. Ironically, I discovered that the process is thrillingly simple . . . as you will discover when you read the verse and follow the steps in the Handbook.

The PeaceFinder was written with love and is presented to you with love. My fondest hope is that this book will make a difference for good. We can no longer bear the bitter consequences of war. It is imperative that we, as members of the global community, join hands and collectively say, "Enough!"

JOAN MCWILLIAMS

Introduction

Never doubt that a small group
of thoughtful, committed citizens
can change the world.
Indeed, it is the only thing
that ever has.

™ MARGARET MEAD

Welcome to the world of *The PeaceFinder: Riley McFee's Quest for World Peace,* and congratulations on your willingness to discover your voice for world peace. Change begins with one person at a time, and you are part of that change!

This book is divided into two parts. The first part is the story of *Riley McFee* and his quest for world peace. The verse will show you how to use your mind, your heart, and your soul to create expectations of peace and let them sail into the universe. You will learn how important it is for all people to participate in this effort. When enough people demand peace, we will create a critical mass, and peace will happen. We have the gifts to change the world, and the poem explains how to do it.

Take time to enjoy the words of the verse as well as the message. It's even better when you read it out loud. If you need further definition of the words, look in the Glossary. It's at the end of the book.

The second part of the book is The Eight Steps to World Peace: A Handbook for PeaceFinders (That's You!). The Handbook provides a more detailed explanation of the principles upon which the verse is based. Some of the principles find their roots in scientific exploration, and some of them reflect common human experiences. They show us how to use our wisdom and imagination to change the world.

The Handbook also contains suggestions for becoming a Peace Participant. It is important to think Peace, but there are actions we can take to support our thoughts and desires. You will find some ideas in "Step Eight." If you want to participate in an organization that promotes peace, you will find some suggestions in the Resource Guide.

Read *The PeaceFinder* and the Handbook with an open mind, an open soul, and an open heart. We are entering a new era that has been born partly out of necessity and partly out of our own greater understanding of the world. The sooner we reject war and violence and demand the peaceful resolution of problems, the sooner we can focus our time, energy, and resources on our survival.

The PeaceFinder

Riley McFee's Quest
for World Peace

THROW OPEN THE DOORS!

Here comes Riley McFee

With dreams for the World and the way things should be.

He has bright red hair and a felicitous smile,

He's a good-natured, virtuous, loveable child.

But his gifts are the things that set him apart:

His mind and his spirit, his soul and his heart.

Riley's mind is exquisite; it sparkles with brilliancy.

He can solve any problem with skill and resiliency.

He can answer most questions with deft flexibility

In a way that confirms his unique credibility.

Riley's spirit, a truly remarkable thing,

Lets him soar to the sky just as though he had wings.

He can travel to planets and skip through space.

He can fly 'round the world and land anyplace

Where people or animals need his brave skills

To help them survive and maintain their free will.

Riley's heart speaks of passion,

of truth, and emotion.

It directs him to act

with both love and devotion.

His soul is the link to the infinite force

That binds humankind to the ultimate source

Of limitless energy, thought, and reflection,

Of seminal power, and earthly perfection.

Riley cherished his gifts; he used them with care
To challenge assumptions that didn't seem fair.
He used them to change both the course and direction
Of life on this earth and the true disaffection
From values that cry out for collaborative unity
And the mindful connection of the global community.

The question that Riley confronted this day

Is one that had caused him substantial dismay.

He searched in his mind but could not understand

Why humans bow mutely and fail to demand

Universal adherence to standards of life

That will bring about peace and the freedom from strife.

"Why," queried Riley, "do people devise

Schemes that will lead to their certain demise?

Is it nature, or demons, or terminal greed,

Or misguided beliefs, or insatiable need

That compel their behavior and make them ignore

Their power to terminate violence and war?

And is there a way to turn things around
So kindness and love can freely abound;
So all human beings can speak with one voice
And loudly declare that world peace is their choice?"

Riley searched for the answer as if on a mission.

He traveled the world full of hope and ambition.

He talked to the Muslims and Christians and Jews.

He spoke with some Buddhists and Hindus he knew.

They said the same thing: "There was nothing to fear."

They wanted world peace—it was priceless and dear.

Yet they could do nothing with words of benevolence

Until all human beings rejected malevolence.

Riley wasn't discouraged; he kept to his task.

He met with world leaders to lay aside masks

Of deception and power, rancor and greed,

In a forum where talks of peace could proceed.

But their egos and politics got in the way.

The commanders-in-chief were unable to stay

On a path that would guide them to worldwide rapport

By which they could obviate violence and war.

The meeting was ended before it began

Without an agreement, consensus, or plan.

Riley started to worry. He needed instruction

To move humankind from the brink of destruction.

He took to the streets; there was no time to lose.

He spoke with the common folk, searching for clues

That would answer his question with patent finality,

"Can all people unite to make peace a reality?"

"No!" said the skeptics;
they shouted frenetically!
"Actually, we have been
altered genetically
By our ancestors' virulent acts
and omissions.
There is scant hope for change
and far less for remission."

"It might be less onerous," one skeptic surmised,

"If the violence and hatred affected the lives

Of only those people who choose to participate.

But it's much worse than that; it wounds and debilitates

Innocent children

And teaches them how, at an early age,

To model their elders' venomous rage."

The skeptics' grave message
filled Riley with gloom.
He felt crushed by a sense
of impending doom.
He knew that the fighting
must be stopped and replaced
With a model of Peace
for the whole human race.

"But this kind of change would require a miracle,
The strength of a giant with knowledge empirical."
Riley needed a hero with wisdom sublime
Who could rescue the world with a new paradigm.

As he pondered the problem, an old woman drew near.

She was wizened and craggy and spoke as a seer.

"Human beings are not doomed, they are merely evolving.

Their gifts make them capable of finally resolving

The disputes, dilemmas, and ancient transgressions

That have thwarted their growth

and stopped their progression."

Riley welcomed the old woman's words of advice.

He agreed with her premise, but would it suffice?

He knew that the woman was clever and wise.

She came in good faith with no pretense or guise.

But her words failed to show him <u>how</u> he could find

The way that each person can save humankind.

Riley started to give up his hopes and his dreams,

His desires, his visions, his trust, and his schemes

When a sprightly young child emerged from the crowd,

And without hesitation, she shouted out loud,

"I can answer your question! I know the way
To bring peace to the earth and hold evil at bay.
We must think with our minds and our souls and our hearts
And communicate thoughts of goodwill as a start."

"With all due respect, this solution seemed ludicrous!
Did this child mean that mere thought is the impetus
To resolve all disputes and bring about peace,
To reconcile nations and cause wars to cease?"

"Yes," said the child, "you may think it's naïve,
But people have skills they are yet to perceive.
Their thoughts and beliefs can direct their experience
And verify once and for all their omniscience."

"Omniscience!" said Riley, "now this is audacious!
Humans are mortals; the idea is fallacious."
"Wrong," said the child, "we have infinite power
To govern all things and force evil to cower."

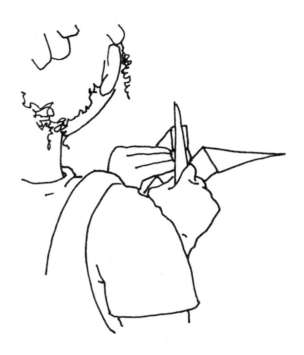

Riley wasn't convinced; he still had some doubts.

Yet what could he lose if he just tried it out?

So he said, "Show me how to use this technique

To join with all people—the strong and the weak—

To renounce and repudiate malice and scorn

And permit a new era of peace to be born."

"It's really quite simple," the child related,

"To reject and rewrite the scripts we've created."

"First, go to the place where your power resides,
Where your soul, your heart, and your mind are allied.
Send love and expect that all violence will cease,
Then fill up your thoughts with emotions of peace.

If reflections of hate or distrust come to mind,
Embrace them, then release them, and leave them behind.
Bring your attention to the clear definition
Of what you expect from your thoughts and volition.

Then give your thoughts wings! Let them fly! Let them sail!

They will carry the message that peace will prevail."

"OK," Riley said, before more time transpired.

"I'll try it; I'll think about what I desire.

I want a world in which peace is the rule,

Where treasured resources are used as the tools

To build friendship and trust and global prosperity

To preserve and protect the world for posterity."

He let this thought go, and a strange thing took place.

His fears and his doubts were serenely replaced

With an unrestrained trust and immutable confidence

That his thought would produce the solicited consequence.

"Oh my gosh!" Riley said. He was taken aback!

For he knew in his mind he was on the right track.

But at the same instant, he knew in his heart

He needed more people to join him and start

To create a collective and critical mass

Of those who are willing to take on the task

Of projecting their thoughts with love and with gratitude

To make peace a habit and make it an attitude.

To accomplish this goal, Riley needed some leaders.

So he turned to his audience—you, the good readers.

"Join with me," he said. "It is easy to start.

Just think with your mind and your soul and your heart.

Now picture a world in which no one is fighting.

All wars have stopped and humankind is uniting

With friendship, accord, and with brave unanimity;

With love and goodwill and with poised equanimity.

Next, add images that express your heart-felt emotions,

Such as rainbows, or hollyhocks, or mountains, or oceans,

Or the unabashed pleasure of those who embrace

A shared vision of peace for the whole human race.

Then let your thoughts fly into time and through space

With absolute trust they will land in a place

Where they will effectively change people's lives

And grandly confirm humankind will survive."

That is all there is to it. The young girl was right.

Riley's heart and his soul sang with joy and delight.

His mind grasped the concept of a timeless connection

Among people who seek a new course and direction.

His spirit was ready to soar and to venture

And take him away to his next great adventure.

Riley left as he came; his mission was finished.

His question was answered; his fears were diminished

By his new understanding that we can control

Our minds and our spirits, our hearts and our souls

To join with all beings in a global revolution

That ensures peace will dominate our next evolution!

So take Riley's message and make the world kinder.

Set your course now as a radiant PeaceFinder.

The
Eight Steps
to World Peace

A Handbook for
PeaceFinders (That's You!)

Introduction

This section of the book explains the ideas and principles upon which *The PeaceFinder* is based. They are remarkably simple, very effective, and will transform your view of the world and your place in the world. You are a PeaceFinder, and peace will happen if you:

1. Open your heart, your mind, and your soul to the possibility that we can achieve world peace. Change your life script. Create a new paradigm.

2. Use your mind and think peace. Visualize a world without war. Believe that it will happen. Expect peace.

3. Think with your heart as well as your mind. Add emotion to your thoughts of peace.

4. Bring soul to your thoughts. Allow your soul to align with your heart and your mind. Focus all your attention on your desire for world peace.

5. Let your thoughts go. Let them fly. Let them sail. Let them carry the message that peace will prevail.

6. Work with the skeptics. Show them how to be open to the possibility that peace can be achieved.

7. Join with other people to create a pandemic of peace. Be the Hundredth Monkey!

8. Be a Peace Participant. Take actions that support your thoughts for peace.

Riley McFee asks the question, "Can all people unite to make peace a reality?" The answer is a resounding YES! It is so simple. We create our reality with our thoughts. Our thoughts become our world. If we use our minds, our hearts, and our souls to expect peace, it will happen!

Join the citizens of the global community. Together we will change the world.

Throw Open the Doors to the Possibility of Peace!

Change Your Script!

Shift Your Paradigm!

Throw Open the Doors to the Possibility of Peace! Change Your Script! Shift Your Paradigm!

*A*s a first step towards peace, throw open the doors of your mind, your heart, and your soul to the idea that peace is attainable. Open yourself to the possibility that we can resolve disputes without violence.

We are evolving as a species, and when we begin to honestly examine the assumptions we make, we will change our life scripts. When we rewrite our scripts, we will replace our world view and change our way of thinking.

Our life scripts are like stories. We start writing them on the day we are born. We receive information, we make decisions based on that information, and we create our reality—our scripts. These scripts change as we receive new information.

Think of an example in your own life. Perhaps you were given information as a child that caused you to form prejudices. The information may have come to you through a bad experience, or it may have been taught to you by your parents. As you grew, you had positive encounters that made you realize that the information on which you based your opinions was not valid. You gained a new perspective and rejected your bias. You changed your script. You saw things in a different way.

When we change the way that we view and react to situations, we experience a paradigm shift. The concept was developed in 1962 by Thomas Kuhn, who wrote *The Structure of Scientific Revolution*. Kuhn believed that scientific advancement involves a "series of peaceful interludes punctuated by intellectually violent revolutions," and in those revolutions, "one conceptual world view is replaced by another." When one view is replaced by another, a paradigm shift occurs, and we understand and respond to challenges in a new way.

It is time to create a paradigm shift by which we, as a global community, reject war and demand peace. This shift will start when we change our life scripts. We have allowed violence to become an integral part of our scripts. We tacitly let it come into our lives. We spoon-feed violence to our children and to ourselves through advertisements, commercials, news programs, cartoons, videos, DVDs, and TV shows. We allow violence to exist in our homes, our communities, and our govenments. Our language is replete with hate-filled phrases. We are scripted to believe that violence is an acceptable means of dispute resolution!

But, it does not have to be that way. When we change our life scripts and replace violence with love and compassion, we will experience a paradigm shift: we will replace our acceptance of war with our expectation of peace. We will respond to global and personal disputes in a new way.

There is an interesting story about Anwar El-Sadat, the former president of Egypt. It is a true story as reported in his autobiography, *In Search of Identity*. It demonstrates how Sadat changed his life script and experienced a paradigm shift.

As a young man, Anwar El-Sadat was imprisoned for many years in the Aliens' Jail and in Cell 54 in the Cairo Central prison. While in prison, Sadat read voraciously, prayed, and meditated. As a result, his "relations with the entire universe began to be reshaped, and love became the fountainhead of all [his] actions and feelings."

Sadat began his imprisonment as a person who hated others, particularly the Israelis. He lived in a society where hate prevailed. Through his ordeal in prison, Sadat changed his script and shifted his paradigm. His transformation was so profound that, when he became the president of Egypt, he drafted a Peace Initiative and delivered it at the Knesset in Jerusalem. Doing so was an unprecedented gesture and ultimately led to the Camp David Accord. It is an amazing story of how one person can move from hate to love.

Can *we* change our scripts and find a path to peace? Actually, we have no choice. Violence and war are options we can no longer afford. We need to spend our time, money, and precious human resources on our survival and on the survival of the planet. We need to turn our focused and united attention to issues of poverty, hunger, illness, environmental depletion, and pollution. The world is one global community, and we need to preserve it for our children and those children who follow.

It's time to take action, and that must start with each one of us. Here are some suggestions. In moments of quiet, take time to honestly examine your life script. Become aware of the role violence plays in your life. Do you casually and mindlessly receive violence as it is presented to you by your friends, your family, the media, or world leaders? Is your acceptance of violence unintended or is it driven by hate? If you are motivated by hate, what is the source? Is your acceptance of violence occasioned by your anger or fear? Whom or what is the object of your anger? Why are you fearful? Are you making decisions that perpetuate violence? Are they misguided? Do you use language that incites violence? What information do you need in order to reject violence and war as problem-solving methods?

Once you examine the source and validity of your life script, you can begin to gather information and make a shift. Step out of your old patterns of thinking and speaking that have been carefully molded by the people or events that have influenced you. See your life and the world as an indivisible whole. You are not separate, and you are not alone. Reject the idea that violence and war are tolerable. Discard negative thoughts. Open yourself to the field of infinite possibility by letting go of preconceived notions, programmed responses, and especially the "we have always done it this way" mode. Feel the positive emotions of gratitude, kindness, courage, love, and peace of mind. Seek truth. Avoid judgments. Forgive yourself and others. Have compassion. Be present. Replace hate with love. Change your life script and shift your paradigm from deep inside. Mahatma Gandhi said, "You must be the change you wish to see in the world."

Now, take a deep breath and pat yourself on the back. Congratulations. You have taken an enormous step!

Use Your Mind!
Think Peace —
Expect Peace!

Use Your Mind!

Think Peace — Expect Peace!

We humans are amazing! In fact, we are miraculous! Just think of the phenomenal power we have. We can create new life. We can heal ourselves and others—even those who are far away. We can solve problems and conjure up memories of past events. We can feel love, hate, anger, joy, and many other emotions. We meditate or pray, and we receive answers. Some of us—for example, Edgar Mitchell, who wrote *The Way of the Explorer: An Apollo Astronaut's Journey Through the Material and Mystical Worlds* and was one of the founders of the Institute of Noetic Science— have even experienced a collective consciousness, a sense that all things in the universe are connected.

Science has unlocked many of the secrets of our incredible power, but, lacking complete scientific answers, humans have historically relied on faith to unravel life's mysteries. Religions have been founded on the miracles that followers experienced. Ancient myths were created to explain universal phenomena. Life practices are guided by events and knowledge gleaned from thoughts and emotions. It would be wonderful to have a definitive scientific explanation for all of our experiences. However, the absence of such answers will not prevent us from continuing to actively participate in life and to savor the miracle of it all.

Think about your own experiences:

- Have you ever thought about an old friend that you had not seen in many years only to have that friend call you?
- Have you ever had a question in your mind, and the answer was presented to you in a book you happened to notice in the bookstore or by a stranger you met quite by chance?
- Have you ever been in a precarious situation and, without fear, you stepped away from it in total safety?
- Have you ever had a sense that you caused something to happen through your intention?
- Have you ever been in a group and had the feeling that the group members were connected by their thoughts or senses?
- Have you read about or experienced a distant healing?

These are not coincidences or chance events. They are examples of the way we create and choose results with our thoughts. Every thought you have affects other people who may be physically near to you or in other parts of the world!

But, can these experiences be explained by scientists? Yes, to a degree. Consciousness studies teach us that our thoughts can be in different places at the same time. Some scientists believe that there is a vast energy source that exists in the universe. As explained by Lynne McTaggart in her book, *The Field: The Quest for the Secret Force of the Universe,* it is called the Zero Point Field and implies that all matter in the universe, including our thoughts, is connected by waves that spread out to infinity. It ties all parts of the universe together.

Studies by Dr. Masaru Emoto, who wrote *The Hidden Messages of Water,* lend support to this concept. Dr. Emoto's experiments demonstrate that our thoughts can physically affect water crystals.

He developed a method by which he shows that water crystals become pure and crystalline when exposed to words like "love" and "peace." No crystals are formed when the water is exposed to phrases like, "I hate you," and "I will kill you." The change in the water crystals occurs even when the words and phrases are in different languages. It occurs when thoughts are sent from locations that are physically distant from the water.

These studies support and explain our experiences. Our thoughts can influence others, even if they are in distant and separate parts of the world. Our thoughts can carry messages and direct global change; they can make anything possible. Anything—including peace.

You can communicate with your thoughts. Put your mind to work and define your expectations. As the young girl in *The PeaceFinder* said, "Bring your attention to the clear definition of what you expect from your thoughts and volition."

Think about what you desire. Be clear about your intention. Focus on that intention because you will create whatever it is that you want. Define your expectation of peace. Don't ask for peace—expect it. And, expect it now, not in the future. We are the leaders. We are the creators. We need only express ourselves.

Your thoughts are your voice for peace. This is how you can join with other people all over the world to make peace happen. You are no longer disenfranchised. You are a participant! When the critical mass is reached, peace will become a habit— an attitude.

STEP THREE

Think
With Your Heart!

Think With Your Heart!

*I*f we want to add power to our messages of peace, we must think not only with our minds but also with our hearts. Our hearts add the juice, the sentiments, and the feelings that support our desired outcome. As it says in the story of *The PeaceFinder*, our hearts speak of passion and truth and emotion. They direct us to act with both love and devotion.

But can we really think with our *hearts*? Absolutely—we always have.

Throughout history people have used their hearts to describe their emotions; their compassion; their harmony; and their feelings of loss, despair, and pain. In *Proverbs* 23:7, we are told that, "We are what we think in our hearts." *Proverbs* 15:13 states that, "Our spirit will be broken by sorrow in our hearts." We sing, "Deep in my heart, I do believe, we shall overcome someday." And, in Antoine de Saint-Exupery's wonderful book, *The Little Prince*, the fox tells us that, "One sees clearly only with the heart. Anything essential is invisible to the eyes."

Expressions of the heart are very common. We say, "Bless his heart," "My heart aches for her," "My heart goes out to you," "That is the heart of the problem," "I love you with all my heart," "Cross my heart and hope to die," and "My heart is broken."

When we are surprised by shocking news, we instinctively put our hand on our heart. We make pledges with our hand on our heart. In his book, *The Heart's Code,* Paul Pearsall describes heart transplant patients who experience the likes and dislikes of their donor even though they never knew the person who gave them the heart.

In yoga, energy centers of the body are defined as chakras. The heart is considered to be one of those energy centers; it is referred to as the fourth chakra, the heart chakra. When it is in balance, practitioners believe that a person can connect with universal love and consciousness.

Experience tells us that we do think with our hearts. By adding the heart's energy and emotions to our thoughts of peace, we add strength and passion to those thoughts. Our "heartfelt" emotions guide and empower our thoughts.

So, as you think peace, add the emotions that you feel: the joy, the happiness, the gratitude, the contentment that will come when people no longer have to worry about violence. Feel the energy of the thought. Take a deep breath, and, as you exhale, let your breath and your thoughts for peace go to your heart. Visualize whatever you feel in a deeply connected way, and add it to your thoughts.

Think with your heart!

Bring Your Soul to Your Thoughts!

Bring Your Soul to Your Thoughts!

*T*he soul is the essence or the nonphysical reality of our being. It links us to the ultimate source of limitless energy and power. The soul has intrinsic spiritual purpose. Many people believe that the soul is the immortal part of our being that survives our death.

Just as we saw with the power of the heart, people throughout history, from the ancient Greeks and Egyptians to modern songwriters, have spoken of the music of the soul.

So, first you must understand that your soul exists and is always on your side. It is the essential core of who you are.

Then:

- Sit quietly at least once a day in a peaceful place where you can be alone. Plan on being uninterrupted.
- With closed eyes, just experience a sense of connectedness and love. Focus on your breath.
- As competing thoughts intrude, embrace them, discard them, and leave them behind.
- Release the thoughts, feelings, and actions of anger.
- Separate yourself from material needs.

- Let thoughts of petty emotions go.
- Feel love and joy.

Clear your soul! Let your soul sparkle! Give it absolute freedom!

In this process you will create a pathway for your soul to connect with your heart and your mind. You are adding the strength of your soul to your thoughts of peace.

Riley says that our hearts and our souls and our minds are allied. They are in concert. They work together. As you think peace, add the emotion of your heart and the power of your soul to your thoughts.

Let Your Thoughts Go.

Give Them Wings —
Let Them Fly!

Let Your Thoughts Go.
Give Them Wings — Let Them Fly!

*T*his is an easy step!

Just spread your arms to the sky and release your thoughts. They will leave you with all the emotion and all the soul that you have given them. They will go into the universe with your message, your trust, and your expectations. They will create your reality.

As the young girl in *The PeaceFinder* says:

"Then give your thoughts wings. Let them fly! Let them sail!
They will carry the message that peace will prevail!"

That's the way the world works. You're releasing your thoughts to the highest good. You become detached from them and let them go. You bring change to the world with your thoughts. You bring peace to the earth.

STEP SIX

Work With
the Skeptics!

Work With the Skeptics!

*A*fter speaking to religious emissaries and world leaders, Riley was unable to find the answer to his question, "Can all people unite to make peace a reality?" So, he took to the streets and started talking to the people there. And whom did he meet? The skeptics! These are the people who will always find a way to discount your dreams and divert you from your search for a better world.

Skeptics will criticize the message of *The PeaceFinder* because it appears to be too simple to work. They may not understand that the simplicity of this process is the key to its success. The skeptics believe that we have been "altered genetically by our ancestor's virulent acts and omissions." The skeptics believe that "there is scant hope for change and far less for remission."

But the old woman says:

"Human beings are not doomed, they are merely evolving.

Their gifts make them capable of finally resolving

The disputes, dilemmas, and ancient transgressions

That have thwarted their growth and stopped their progression."

There is no doubt that we carry the burden of a history of violence. Even today, the world's children—our children—continue to be emotionally, spiritually, and physically devastated by violence.

But what can we do? If we follow the skeptics, we will concede that change is not possible. We will continue to meet violence with violence just as it has been taught to us. Reliance on our governments doesn't work because governmental institutions are designed to protect only the interests of their constituents—their citizens—in whatever way they might interpret that mandate. Religious organizations should be able to help and many of them do. However, like many organizations, religions get bogged down with bureaucratic red tape and political issues. Many wars have been fought in the name of religion. Ultimately, as Albert Einstein said, "We cannot solve our problems with the same thinking we used when we created them."

The only answer is to shift our paradigms and reject the idea that we have to manipulate others to gain power. Coercion is not the answer because it causes insecurity, anger, fear, and conflict. As Sadat stated in his book, *In Search of Identity*, power-based communities are inconsistent with our nature. They are built on hate and cannot survive. Hate and violence create more problems than they solve.

We cannot control the skeptics, but we can control our attitude and the manner in which we participate in the peace process. We can be an example for the skeptics and show them how to create peace.

So, become an influence for peace. Focus on communicating love and joy. Embrace the skeptics. Acknowledge the pain that we have inflicted and seek universal forgiveness. Stop judging. Show mercy. On a daily basis, strive to maintain the universal connection with all creatures. When enough people think and live peace, the skeptics will join.

Be the
Hundredth Monkey!

Be the Hundredth Monkey!

When Riley McFee learns that his thoughts are the key to establishing world peace, he comes to another important conclusion. He realizes that he can't do it alone. He needs the help of his readers; he needs the help of people all over the world. To make a global change, he needs a "collective and critical mass of those who are willing to take on the task of projecting their thoughts with love and with gratitude to make peace a habit and make it an attitude."

Violence will stop only when the citizens of the world insist on it. When enough people demand new and better solutions, we will create a critical mass, and peace will become a global habit—an expectation.

The story of the Hundredth Monkey demonstrates how this phenomenon works. Ken Keyes, Jr., an award-winning author and peace advocate, noted that scientists had been studying the Japanese monkey, *Macaca fuscata*, for over thirty years. The monkeys lived on geographically distant islands. In 1952, scientists began to give sweet potatoes to the monkeys on the island of Koshima. The monkeys liked the sweet potatoes, but they did not like the sand on them.

A young monkey named Imo discovered that she could wash the sweet potato in a nearby stream. She taught her mother this trick.

Her playmates also learned the new way and taught their mothers. As the scientists watched, other monkeys learned to wash their potatoes in the stream until, over a six-year period, all of the young monkeys followed this pattern and many of the adults imitated their children.

Then, one day, when the "ninety-ninth" monkey began to wash her sweet potato, the hundredth monkey joined the group, and the added energy of the hundredth monkey created a breakthrough. By that evening, almost all of the monkeys in the colony were washing their potatoes. The critical mass had been reached.

But, that is not the end of the story. Without any means of known communication, monkeys on distant islands also began to wash their potatoes. This remarkable event implies that the idea of washing the potatoes was communicated by the first monkeys merely through the thought process. The idea was communicated mind to mind!

The Hundredth Monkey is a wonderful story about the power of individual beings. One monkey saw a solution and implemented it. Others followed. Soon, the behavior was embraced by additional monkeys because it made sense. The monkeys didn't ask for approval. They didn't seek the advice and consent of their leaders. They just did it!

This phenomenon is beautifully explained in *The Tipping Point* by Malcolm Gladwell. Mr. Gladwell defines the Tipping Point as "that magic moment when an idea, trend, or social behavior crosses a threshold, tips, and spreads like wildfire." A social trend, for example, may start slowly until there are enough people (the critical mass) who embrace the idea. When that happens, the trend "tips," and it becomes an accepted part of the social fabric.

This will happen with peace, and it is the moment that we are seeking. It will be the point in time when enough people in the world reject violence and war and make peace an expectation—a habit.

We will reach that moment. Join the search for peaceful solutions. Others are. Look at the eight million Iraqis who in 2005 went to the voting booths in spite of being threatened with their lives. Look at the heroic efforts and sacrifices that the Israelis and Palestinians are making to bring peace to that region. These are difficult transitions, and we cannot know whether these efforts will be sustained. However, they are a start. People are on the move. We must unite with them.

Join the movement! Be creative, be open, be aware. Add your thoughts of peace to the millions of others that will be projected. Share your intentions and your aspirations. Search for magical and miraculous answers. We do not know when the critical mass will be reached. But, as we accumulate our acts and our thoughts, we will be adding and adding and adding to the collective awakening. And then it will happen! The sheer mass will tip, and we will have enduring peace.

Don't give up. Be a part of the critical mass. Who knows? You might be the Hundredth Monkey!!

STEP EIGHT

Be a
Peace Participant!

Be a Peace Participant!

$\mathcal{W}$hile the most important lesson of *The PeaceFinder* is to think Peace, there are also actions you can take to support your peace thoughts. Be a Peace Participant. You can:

1. Start a Riley McFee Peace Group.

Are you a member of a book club, study group, prayer circle or some other group that meets regularly? Make *The PeaceFinder* a study topic. If you are not a member of such a group, gather your friends together and start your own Riley McFee Peace Group.

 You may want to:

- Read the poem, *The PeaceFinder*, out loud.

- Discuss your thoughts about violence and world peace.

- Talk about your dreams for the world.

- Send love and thoughts of peace to the people who attend your group.

- Ask members to follow the guidelines of *The PeaceFinder*.

- Send thoughts of peace to the people of the world.

Be sure to support the participation of the people in your group. Listen for the meaning behind their words. Create a trusting and supportive environment. Give every person an equal hearing. Look beyond your preconceived ideas. Focus on your common aspiration of peace. Once you forget about your personal agenda and join with other members to focus on the goal of the group, you will experience the collective consciousness of the group. This is a treasure. Embrace it. Use the collective leadership to create peace.

Once a month, extend your Peace Group by asking members to invite their friends to the circle.

2. Make and Distribute Origami Peace Cranes— A Symbol of International Peace.

Symbols are models or characters that have universal meaning. They represent certain qualities or traits, and when we see them, we instinctively know their values and what they represent. The origami peace crane is a symbol that will remind us to send thoughts of peace.

According to Japanese legend, anyone who makes 1,000 of these paper cranes will be granted a wish for health and peace.

This legend became prominent when a girl from Hiroshima, Japan, Sadako Sasaki, contracted leukemia after the atom bomb was dropped on her city on August 6, 1945. Sadako's friend suggested that she start making paper cranes so that, when she reached 1,000, her wish for health and peace would be fulfilled. Sadako never stopped making the cranes but, in 1955, before she could make 1,000 cranes, she died at the age of twelve.

Sadako was an inspiration. Her classmates decided to build a monument to her and to all the children who died from the atom bomb. In 1958, a statue of Sadako holding a golden crane was unveiled in the Hiroshima Peace Park. The inscription on the statue reads:

"This is our cry, This is our prayer,
Peace in the World."

Since then, children and adults from all over the world have sent or taken paper cranes to the Hiroshima Peace Park. They are hung on the statue of Sadako.

From this poignant beginning, the paper crane has become an international symbol of peace. A wonderful children's peace statue was created by school children in Albuquerque, New Mexico. It took five years and was built with donations from children in 63 countries and all 50 of the United States. The statue resides temporarily in Santa Fe, New Mexico and is decorated with paper cranes that are sent from all over the world. There is also a Sadako statue in Seattle, Washington.

School children in Sydney, Australia folded paper cranes and hung them on a "Wishing Tree." A Girl Scout troop in Adel, Georgia, USA made 1,000 paper cranes and delivered them to nursing homes, businesses, schools, churches, family, and friends during the Christmas season to spread the message of World Peace. As Sadako had done, they wrote the word, "PEACE," on the wings of the crane.

In December 2004, the Thai government dropped one hundred million paper cranes from planes over the southern provinces of that country in support of peace in that region. The birds were folded by millions of people throughout Thailand. Messages of peace were written on the wings. The prime minister signed some of the birds, and those who found his cranes were promised a job or a scholarship. The governor of one province promised a bicycle to residents who picked up 50,000 cranes. It was a huge event.

Making peace cranes is a way to communicate our thoughts of peace to people all over the world. Each one is a prayer for peace. Learn to make paper cranes. Here's how:

1. Start with a square piece of paper. Fold the paper diagonally to form a triangle. Unfold the paper.

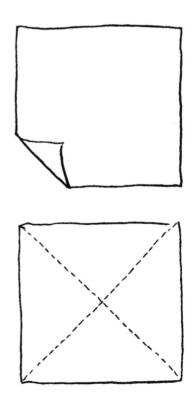

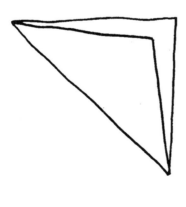

2. Now fold the paper diagonally in the other direction. Unfold the paper and turn it over.

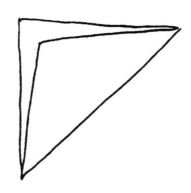

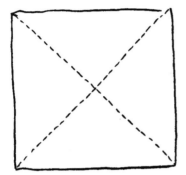

3. Fold the paper in half to the "east" to form a rectangle. Unfold the paper. Now fold the paper in half to the "north" to form a new rectangle.

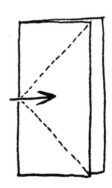

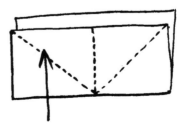

4. Unfold the paper, but don't flatten it out.

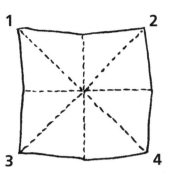

5. Bring all four corners of the paper together, one at a time. You will make a flat square. This square has an open end where all four corners of the paper come together. It has two flaps on the right and two flaps on the left.

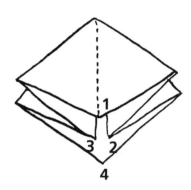

6. Lift the upper **right** flap and fold it in the direction of the arrow. Crease along line **a–c**. Then lift the upper **left** flap and fold in the direction of the arrow. Crease along line **a–b**.

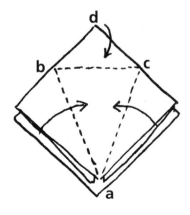

7. Lift the paper at point **d** and fold down the triangle **bcd**. Crease along line **b–c**.

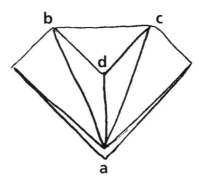

8. Undo the three folds you just made (steps 6 and 7), and your paper will have the crease lines shown at right. Then lift just the top layer of the paper at point **a**. Open it up and back to line **b–c**. Crease the line **b–c**.

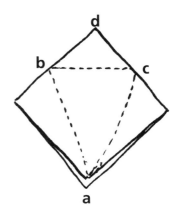

9. Press on points **b** and **c** to reverse the folds along lines **a–b** and **a–c**. The trick is to get the paper to lie flat in the long diamond shape. Keep trying. It will work.

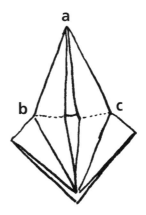

10. Turn the paper over. Repeat Steps 6–9 on this side. When you have finished, your paper will look like this diamond with two "legs" at the bottom. Taper the diamond at its legs by folding the top layer of each side in the direction of the arrows along lines **a–f** and **a–e** so that they meet in the center. Flip the paper over and repeat the same thing to complete the tapering of the two legs.

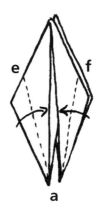

11. This figure has two skinny legs. Lift the upper flap at point **f** (**be sure it's just the upper flap**), and fold it over in the direction of the arrow—just like you are turning the page of a book. This is called a "book fold." Flip the figure over and repeat the "book fold." Be sure to fold over only the top "page."

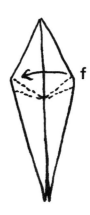

12. This figure looks like a fox with two pointy ears at the top and a pointy nose at the bottom. Open the upper layer of the fox's mouth at point **a**, and crease it along line **g–h** so that the fox's nose touches the top of the fox's ears. Turn the figure over and repeat this step on the other side so that all four points touch.

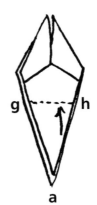

13. Now for another "book fold." Lift the top layer (at point **f**), and fold it in the direction of the arrow. Flip the figure over and repeat the "book fold" on this side.

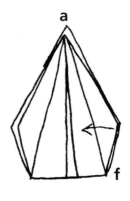

14. There are two points, **a** and **b**, below the upper flap. Pull out each one, in the direction of the arrows, as far as shown. Press down along the base (at points **x** and **y**) to make them stay in place.

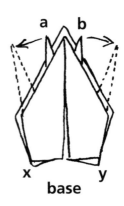

15. Take the end of one of the points, and bend it down to make the head of the crane. Using your thumbnail, reverse the crease in the head, and pinch it to form the beak. The other point becomes the tail.

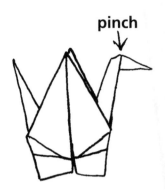

pinch

16. Open the body by blowing into the hole underneath the crane, and then gently pull out the wings. Voila! You have made a peace crane!

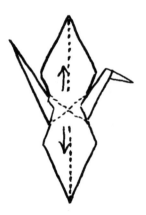

Write peace messages on the wings of your cranes. Give them to friends. Use them as gift wrapping decorations. Hang them on your trees. Make a mobile. Display them in a mall. Hang them in your sports arena. Let them represent the message of *The PeaceFinder*. They are the international symbol of peace!

3. Create a Peace Park.

Peace Parks are literally springing up all over the world. There are Peace Parks in the United States, Scotland, South Africa, the Philippines, Tanzania, Italy, and Jamaica. Some are created in an effort to stop conflict between nations. Others are designed to preserve the environment. Peace Parks do not solve all of the international problems, but they are part of the solution, and they are certainly consistent with the message of *The PeaceFinder*: think peace, participate in peace.

If this idea appeals to you, find or create a Peace Park design with which you are comfortable. It doesn't have to be a huge project. It might be so simple as planting a tree in a botanic garden or park where school children can hang their origami peace cranes. Perhaps your local college or university will support the creation of a peace garden. Or, you may want to check with your city officials to see if an existing park could be rededicated as a peace park. Wonderful bronze sculptures have been created for some of these parks, and you might include that in your planning.

Getting the money to support your project requires only creativity and tenacity. Here are some suggestions:

- Start a "penny campaign" and enlist the support of your local school district. Ask each child in the district to bring a penny. The campaign could be coordinated with peace studies or the story of Sadako.

- Ask the churches, temples, mosques, and community centers in your city to celebrate a "Peace Day" with special donations going to your peace project.

- Support and publicize a peace walk.

- Ask people to give donations to the peace park project in place of wedding, Christmas, Chanukah, christening or bar mitzvah gifts. Include a statement on your invitations that guests are encouraged to donate to the Peace Park project in lieu of gifts. Send the donor a thank you note and a peace crane.

- Help your children design money-making projects. Julia, a student in Denver, Colorado, raised $500 through a bake sale she organized at her school. Perhaps local merchants would allow your children to set up lemonade stands in front of their stores. Or, children could make peace cranes and sell them.

- Ask local theatre groups to stay after the performance and give autographs (or paper cranes) in exchange for donations.

- Budget your wedding or other celebration then cut the budget by ten percent. Have a smaller, less extravagant affair, and give the ten percent that you saved to the Peace Park project.

- Organize a Peace Day celebration with music, arts and crafts, and ethnic performances. Donate all proceeds to the Peace Park project.

- Contact professional organizations such as Kiwanis, Rotary, the Girl/Boy Scouts, fraternities/sororities, chambers of commerce, civic clubs—and try to get their volunteer and financial support for the project. Don't forget local businesses.

- Apply for grants from foundations or your state lottery association.

- To build grassroots support in addition to the above, contact civic leaders, military establishments, schools, colleges and universities, churches, senior citizens organizations, conservation organizations, historic preservation organizations, and park and garden organizations.

Next, enlist committee members, draw up your plan, and go for it. You can make it happen! This is a major contribution to your community, the country, and the world. Dare to be remarkable! Dare to make a difference!

4. Become an Activist for Peace.

An "activist" is a person who engages in vigorous action. The action may be overt, such as participating in peace activities. Or, it may be a private activity, such as helping to mentor a child or contributing to a peace organization.

 Here are some suggestions:

- Focus on your children and give them unqualified love and attention. Do not teach them violence by your behavior. Don't allow violent music, TV, or movies in your home. Monitor the TV shows (including the commercials), the movies and the DVDs they watch.

- Volunteer as a child's mentor in your neighborhood school, your church, or your neighborhood.

- Practice respect and nonjudgmental love. Be aware of the words you use and raise the level of your language.

- Write letters to world leaders.

- Become a peace advocate in your community.

- Do not support violent TV programs, advertisements, movies, DVDs, CDs or videos.

- Be mindful of ways you can help others and offer them your help.

- Learn a new language.

- Study different cultures.

- Give lectures on peace.

- Join a peace organization.

- Take a walk. Enjoy the blue sky, the trees, the streams. Breath deeply and connect with nature.

- Find your passion. Find your mission.

Carry the torch! Every voice makes a difference!

5. Contribute to Peace Organizations.

There are many ways you can contribute to peace organizations. You can devote your time and energy to the effort. Or you can contribute money. You will find a list of organizations in the Resource Guide that follows.

6. Look for Opportunities to Make Peace a Habit.

There are numerous ways to help businesses and communities change their scripts and experience a paradigm shift; we just have to notice them. For example, have you ever stopped by a local bookstore and asked how to find their section on "peace"? They probably won't have one! It's hard to imagine that bookstores, which have a myriad of different sections, would not have one section on peace. You can start asking for this. Go to the manager. Make a difference.

As you focus on peace, you will find many opportunities to change society. Be vigilant and help people and businesses change their priorities.

Be a change agent!

7. Change the Priorities of Our Governments.

In 2001, U.S. Representative Dennis J. Kucinich, a Congressman from Ohio, proposed that the government create a cabinet level Department of Peace! The mission of this new department would be to "make non-violence the central organizing principle in our society, advancing human relations in domestic as well as in foreign policy." The Bill never made it out of the committees to which it was referred, but it will be reintroduced.

What a novel idea! Can you imagine what would happen if every country created a Department of Peace, and they actually communicated with one another?

To read about Rep. Kucinich's project, contact: <u>www.house.gov/kucinich/action/peace.htm</u> If you like the idea, write to him. Volunteer. Help create a Department of Peace in your government!

8. Use the Web.

 The world-wide web is an amazing tool, and you can use your email to send your thoughts of peace.

Start by sending a letter to your friends. Ask them to forward it to their friends, and so on.

Your letter might reflect your thoughts for peace, or it may support a particular cause, such as an appeal to the United Nations or your congressman.

The ways in which you can use the web are limitless.

What are some of your ideas?

Resource Guide

*Y*ou may be looking for a way to actively participate in an organization that promotes peace and survival. There are literally thousands of them. This section of the book lists both grassroots and large organizations.

This list is neither an endorsement nor a political statement. It is merely a guide to help you find a group that will appreciate your participation and share in your thoughts of peace. Here are some suggestions:

1. The Carnegie Endowment for International Peace

The Carnegie Endowment for International Peace was founded in 1910. It is a private, nonprofit organization dedicated to advancing cooperation between nations and promoting active international engagement by the United States. Endowment associates shape fresh policy approaches through research, publishing, convening, and on occasion, creating new institutions and international networks.

The Carnegie Endowment website is www.ceip.org

2. The Carter Center

The Carter Center, in partnership with Emory University, is committed to advancing human rights and alleviating unnecessary human suffering. It was founded in 1981 by former U.S. President Jimmy Carter and his wife, Rosalynn.

The Carter Center supports worldwide Peace Programs including The Global Development Initiative and The Conflict Resolution Program.

Please contact the Carter Center at www.cartercenter.org

3. The Dr. Laura Schlessinger Foundation

The mission of the Dr. Laura Schlessinger Foundation is to provide powerful advocacy on behalf of abused, abandoned, and neglected children in the United States and Canada. One of the foundation's programs is the My Stuff™ bags. The bags are filled with things a child needs and wants, such as toys, toiletries, a teddy bear, and a blanket. The bags are delivered to children.

To learn more, go to www.drlaura.com

4. For All Kids Foundation

Established in 1997 by Rosie O'Donnell, the For All Kids Foundation helps support the intellectual, social, and cultural development of at-risk and underserved children in the United States.

Their website is www.forallkids.org

5. Oprah's Angel Network

Oprah's Angel Network is a 501(C)(3) organization that was started by Oprah Winfrey to help programs in the United States and the children in Africa. In 2002, Winfrey and a team of volunteers went to Africa to bring hope and Christmas joy to 50,000 South African children.

For more information, go to her website at www.oprah.com

6. Peace Games

Peace Games was founded in 1996 and appears on the Ellen Degeneres website. Volunteers work with children to teach them the skills of cooperation and conflict resolution. It was founded on the belief that young people have the power and responsibility to change the world.

Their website is www.peacegames.org

7. Seeking Common Ground

Seeking Common Ground was co-founded in 1994 by Melodye Feldman, the current Executive Director. SCG brings young Israeli, Palestinian, and American women together for a year-long intensive program to engage in activities that promote peace and the status and empowerment of women.

To learn more, go to www.s-c-g.org.

8. sponsorKIDS®

sponsorKIDS® was founded by Jeannette Kravitz. One of the programs of sponsorKIDS® is Peace Journey, which guides global friendships among the children of the world by sponsoring groups of students and teachers on trips to foreign countries on a mission of cultural exploration.

sponsorKIDS® can be reached at http://peacejourney.com

9. The United States Institute of Peace

Established in 1984, the United States Institute of Peace is an independent, nonpartisan federal institution created by Congress to promote the prevention, management, and peaceful resolution of international conflicts. The institute supports research grants, fellowships, professional training, educational programs, conferences, workshops, library services, and publications.

The institute's website address is www.usip.org

10. Additional Suggestions

If you do a general search on the web using the word "peace," you will be amazed at the number of sites you will find. I discovered 289,000,000! There are 48,100,000 sites under the search, "peace groups." As you are aware, we have no way of knowing whether all of the sites are legitimate, so you need to research them well before getting involved. However, it is likely that you can find the type of group in which you would like to participate.

The good news is that millions of people are thinking about peace!

Glossary

The poem, *The PeaceFinder*, is made up of wonderful words. Enjoy them. Read them out loud. Listen to them. Take them in, make them your own.

Some of the words may be new to you. If you need to find their meaning, look them up in the Glossary that follows.

Glossary

Aback – by surprise
Abound – be plentiful, thrive
Accomplish – succeed, to complete
Accord – agreement, harmony
Adherence – loyalty, faithfulness
Affirm – avow, proclaim
Allied – united
Ambition – desire, purpose
Ancestor – forefather
Ancient – long past, remote
Assumptions – beliefs
Assure – to make certain
Audacious – outrageous
Bay – at a distance
Benevolence – kindness, compassion
Bow – give in, surrender
Brilliancy – having keen, quick mental abilities
Brink – edge
Cease – stop
Chagrin – shame, embarrassment
Cherished – to treat with affection
Coercion – forcible control or threats
Collaborative – cooperative
Collective – a number of people acting as a group
Commanders-in-chief – leaders
Communicate – share ideas, declare
Compel – force, require
Confidence – trust, certainty
Consensus – general agreement

Consequence – result, outcome
Convinced – sure
Cower – crouch in fear
Credibility – trustworthiness
Critical – indispensable, essential
Craggy – jagged, ragged
Dear – precious, cherished
Debilitates – weakens
Deception – deceit, trickery
Demise – death
Demons – evil beings
Devise – think up, invent
Devotion – dedication, commitment
Dilemmas – problems
Disaffection – separation
Dismay – distress
Diminished – lessened, made smaller
Disputes – arguments, disagreements
Doomed – hopeless
Effectively – having an intended effect
Ego – self-admiration
Elder – an older member of a family or community
Embrace – accept, adopt
Emerge – to come forward
Emotion – strong feelings
Empirical – practical, first-hand
Endurable – lasting
Equanimity – calmness, steadiness
Era – age, period of time
Evolving – developing
Exquisite – precious, matchless
Fallacious – incorrect, false

Felicitous – happy, joyful
Flexibility – adaptability
Forum – place for discussions
Frenetically – excitedly
Genetically – by genes or heredity
Global – worldwide, universal
Gratitude – thankfulness
Guise – pretense
Hesitation – reluctance, uncertainty
Infinite – limitless, without end
Immutable – lasting, enduring
Impending – about to take place
Impetus – momentum, moving force
Infinite – boundless, limitless
Insatiable – not able to be satisfied
Ludicrous – absurd, crazy
Malevolence – hatred, ill-will
Malice – hatred
Mass – a unified group
Mindful – conscious, thoughtful
Misguided – wrong, in error
Mission – quest, assignment
Mortal – subject to death
Mutely – unwilling or unable to speak
Naïve – innocent, unsophisticated
Notion – thought, idea
Obviate – do away with
Omissions – things that have been left out
Omniscience – all-knowing
Onerous – burdensome
Paradigm – model, archetype
Passion – enthusiasm, rapture, fervor

Patent – obvious, apparent
Perceive – recognize
Poised – balanced
Posterity – future generations
Premise – idea, thesis
Pretension – self-importance, showing off
Prevail – succeed, triumph, win
Progression – progress
Projecting – to send out into space
Prosperity – well-being
Queried – asked
Rancor – hostility, antagonism
Rapport – fellowship
Reconcile – reunite, restore to friendship
Reject – turn away from, dismiss
Release – to let go
Remission – relief from, decrease
Renounce – to give up on, to abandon
Repudiate – reject
Resides – lives
Resiliency – ability to move swiftly
Resolving – finding the solution to
Revolution – a complete change
Rewrite – to write again
Scant – little
Scorn – disregard, disdain
Script – life story
Seer – wise person
Seminal – primary
Serenely – calmly
Skeptic – unbeliever, critic
Solicited – that which was requested

Sprightly – full of spirit, lively
Standards – guidelines, principles
Strife – bitter conflict
Sublime – noble, grand, awe-inspiring
Substantial – large, significant
Suffice – satisfy, be sufficient
Surmised – guessed, supposed
Suspicion – distrust
Technique – procedure
Terminal – deadly, fatal
Terminate – stop
Thwarted – stopped, obstructed
Transgressions – sins, misdeeds
Transpired – passed, went by
Ultimate – of the greatest significance
Unabashed – fearless, confident
Unanimity – agreement, unity
Unbridled – unrestrained, free
Unite – to bring together
Universal – existing everywhere
Venomous – poisonous, deadly
Verify – prove, substantiate
Virtuous – honorable, good
Virulent – deadly, lethal
Vision – a mental image
Volition – conscious choice, will
Voracious – greedy, ravenous
Will – desire, purpose
Wisdom – insight, common sense
Wizened – shriveled, wrinkled

Acknowledgements

My special thanks and love go to my wonderful daughters, Jeanette Killip and Kendall Cady, and to my dear sister, Marybeth Starzel. They were there from the start of this book and never hesitated to offer any help they could. Thank you.

The earliest drafts of my manuscript were brilliantly critiqued by a wonderful author, Maria Katzenbach. I also owe my enormous thanks to my family and friends who offered patient and endearing support: My sweet mother, Doreen Harcourt, Jeff Killip, Jack Spiller, the Starzel/Secrest clan, the John Harcourt family, the Ed McWilliams family, John and Pam Moye, Diane Hartman, Stephanie Kane, Jim Lyons, Mark Meyer, Mimi Garrison, Robin Hoffman, Cathie Campbell, Hon. and Mrs. David Ebel, Hon. and Mrs. Carlos Lucero, Hon. Deanell Tacha, Rick Wedgle, Dr. Susan Mason, Dr. Parker Oborn, Martha Hatch, Dr. Dana Cogan, Lynn Luhnow, Mark and Nancy Leonard, Gina Weitzenkorn, and Jacki Wallace.

Shannon Parish, my wonderful illustrator, was a joy and an inspiration. Authors Judith Briles, Mary Jo Fay, Mike Daniels, and Barbara Munson took the time to offer their very professional suggestions, and Alan Bernhard and Alan Stark at the Boulder Bookworks helped put it all together.

Thank you all.

Bibliography

de Saint-Exupery, A., *The Little Prince* (Florida: Harcourt, Inc., 1943).

El-Sadat, A., *In Search of Identity, an Autobiography* (New York: Harper & Row Publishers, 1977, 1978).

Emoto, M., *The Hidden Messages of Water* (Oregon: Beyond Words Publishing, Inc., 2004).

Gladwell, M., *The Tipping Point: How Little Things Can Make a Big Difference* (New York: Back Bay Books/Little, Brown and Company, 2000, 2002).

Kuhn, T., *The Structure of Scientific Revolution* (Chicago: University of Chicago Press, 1962).

McTaggart, L., *The Field: The Quest for the Secret Force of the Universe* (New York: Harper Collins, 2002).

Mitchell, E., *The Way of the Explorer: An Apollo Astronaut's Journey Through the Material and Mystical Worlds* (London: G. P. Putnam, 1996).

Pearsall, P., *The Heart's Code* (New York: Broadway Books, 1998).